Who Was Salvador Dalí?

by Paula K. Manzanero

illustrated by Gregory Copeland

Penguin Workshop

For Ignacio—PM

PENGUIN WORKSHOP
An imprint of Penguin Random House LLC, New York

First published in the United States of America by Penguin Workshop,
an imprint of Penguin Random House LLC, New York, 2023

Visit us online at penguinrandomhouse.com.

Library of Congress Cataloging-in-Publication Data is available.

Printed in the United States of America

ISBN 9780448489568 (paperback)   10 9 8 7 6 5 4 3   WOR
ISBN 9780593661512 (library binding)   10 9 8 7 6 5 4 3 2 WOR

Contents

Who Was
Salvador Dalí?

A well-dressed man with a cane walks up the stairs of the Paris Metro (the underground subway). His hair is windblown, and his mustache is combed just right. As he stares directly into a photographer's camera, a group of Parisians stop to look at him. Or, more accurately, at the large, hairy anteater he is walking at the end of a rope.

Salvador Dalí was already a celebrity when the photo of him was taken in 1969. He was a world-famous painter who was known for using an image of one thing to stand in for something else. This is called symbolism. He was also famous for his unique way of life and his mustache, which he wore thin and styled so that each of the outer tips pointed upward on either side of his nose. Salvador had a friend he had nicknamed "the anteater." Maybe he was creating a tribute to his friend by walking a real anteater? Or maybe he was just being himself.

As a boy, he had been determined to prove he was different. And over the course of his long life, he demonstrated how special he was in every way he could think of. He became a painter, a filmmaker, a writer, a sculptor, and more.

And it turns out that the photographer didn't catch the appearance of a man in a suit with an unexpected animal on a busy city street by accident. This unusual scene was actually planned well in advance. Like social media influencers today, Salvador knew how to set up the right shot at the right angle at the right time. He knew how to get people talking about him and his art. And he loved shocking people.

Salvador was one of the most famous and distinctive artists of the twentieth century. Like his art, his personality was exciting and bold. He enjoyed it when people questioned his unusual style. He wanted them to realize that some works of art, just like some people, require a closer look.

CHAPTER 1
A Life in Spain

Salvador Dalí, whose full name was Salvador Felipe Jacinto Dalí y Domènech, was born on May 11, 1904, in the town of Figueres (say: fee-GER-es), Spain. The town sits in the northeast corner of the country, in Catalonia, close to the

French border. His mother was named Felipa Domènech i Ferrés. His father, Salvador Dalí Cusi, was a lawyer who could sometimes be very strict. The family, which included Salvador's grandmother as well as his aunt Catalina, spoke the Catalan language.

Just nine months before Salvador was born, his older brother, who had also been named Salvador, had died of a stomach flu or infection just before his second birthday. The second Salvador was given his brother's clothes to wear and his toys to play with. In some ways, his parents treated him like another version of their firstborn son, who was no longer with them.

When Salvador was three years old, his sister, Anna Maria, was born. A year later, he started school. By the time Salvador was six, his parents had moved him to a private school, and he also took classes in French, the language he would use throughout most of his adult life.

But Salvador was never very interested in school and wished he could spend his time drawing. While in class, he often stared out the window or up at the ceiling and daydreamed.

He looked at the clouds or the cracks in the paint in the classroom and found hidden shapes and imagined details that were much more appealing to him than his lessons.

His mother encouraged her son's interest in art from a very early age. Her grandfather had been an artistic man who crafted beautiful hair combs, fans, and walking sticks. And she saw some of that creativity in her own son.

Unlike the other students in his class, Salvador wore blue sailor suits to school and shoes with silver buttons. He sometimes even carried a small cane! Now that he was older, he liked to dress up and look fancy. It was important to him that he would never be compared to, or mistaken for, the firstborn Salvador. He didn't mind being different or standing out, as long as he could be himself.

In 1912, when he was eight, the family moved to a house that was big enough for Salvador to set up his own art studio in an old laundry room in the attic. It was here that—in addition to drawing—Salvador began practicing winking and smiling. He said to himself, "Salvador Dalí! You know it now! If you play at being a genius, you'll become one!" Even at this age, his father saw how creative the young daydreamer was. He said, "I have a son who pays not the slightest heed to reality." His father worried that Salvador would grow up to be an artist rather than something more respectable, like a teacher or a lawyer.

Around this time, Salvador painted his first landscape (an image of outdoor scenery) of the town of Figueres using oil paint on a piece of cardboard. This painting, called *Landscape*, shows cypress trees, red rooftops, and birds in the sky. Salvador's early images were of his hometown and the fishing village of Cadaqués (say: ka-da-KES), where his family spent their summer vacations. Salvador loved the rocky coastline and the boats docked in the port of Cadaqués.

Landscape by Dalí, 1914

In Cadaqués, Salvador found his first mentor in family friend Ramon Pichot. (A mentor is someone with skills and experience in a certain subject who trains or advises another person.) Pichot was a painter who worked in the impressionist style, developed in France during the second half of the nineteenth century. The impressionist painters used a broad and rapid style, with brushstrokes that are easily seen and colors that are often bright. They tried to capture the impression—or feeling—of a moment in time rather than a realistic image of their subjects. Ramon Pichot assured Salvador's father that art was the right path for his talented son.

Ramon Pichot

At age twelve, Salvador attended the Figueres Institute, which was like an American high school, intended to prepare him for a future career. His father also enrolled him at the Municipal Drawing School. There, Salvador took drawing lessons from Juan Nuñez Fernandez, who saw how talented Salvador was. He thought the young boy could become a successful painter. And that was the only thing Salvador had ever wanted to do. Now his entire family believed in his talent and his dream. Just one year later, in 1917, Salvador's father organized a show of his drawings at their home.

CHAPTER 2
The Beginnings of an Artist

Although Juan Nuñez Fernandez and Salvador's family gave him their full support, Salvador believed that he needed to *look* like an artist before he could become one. He grew his hair long and practiced making faces in front of the mirror.

Salvador's painting began to show the influence of his friend Ramon Pichot and the impressionist painters. When he was around fourteen years old, he painted *The Woman with the Pitcher*, a work whose light and color are directly in the impressionist style.

Leonardo da Vinci

Although Salvador was becoming more familiar with modern painters of his time, he admired the painters who were known as the old masters—artists who worked in Europe before 1800 and included Rembrandt, Leonardo da Vinci, Michelangelo, Johannes Vermeer, and Diego Velázquez. In 1919, when he was fifteen years old, Salvador wrote an essay about Leonardo da Vinci stating that he thought da Vinci was "the greatest master of painting, a soul that knew how to study, to invent, to create with ardor [love], passion, and energy." And when he was finally able to grow a mustache, it was partly in tribute to the great Spanish master Velázquez.

That same year, Salvador's work was part of a group exhibition, or showing, held in the lobby of Figueres's Municipal Theater. This was his first public show!

Figueres Municipal Theater

Although this was an exciting time for Salvador, in 1921 he experienced a deep tragedy. His mother died of cancer after being sick for only a short while. Salvador was devastated.

Diego Velázquez (1599–1660)

Diego Rodríguez de Silva y Velázquez was born in Seville, Andalusia, Spain. He began training to become a painter when he was around twelve years old. One of the first artists to paint realistic still-life kitchen scenes, Velázquez went on to paint religious images as well as portraits. He used a style of dramatic illumination, showing a high contrast, or difference, between the light and dark parts of his paintings.

Velázquez became the painter for King Philip IV of Spain and completed many portraits of other members of the royal family. The most famous of these is *Las Meninas (The Ladies-in-waiting)*, completed in 1656. It includes a portrait of young Princess Margarita Teresa as well as the reflected portraits of King Philip IV and Mariana of Austria, seen in a mirror above the princess's head.

Velázquez is remembered as the leading artist of the Spanish Golden Age, which lasted from 1492 to 1681.

When his father married his aunt Catalina, Salvador grew much closer to his then-fourteen-year-old sister, Anna Maria. A self-portrait, completed around this time, shows a serious seventeen-year-old Salvador with long sideburns, long hair, and a comically long neck.

In 1922, Salvador began studying at the Royal Academy of Fine Arts of San Fernando in Madrid. He moved into a room at the students' residence.

Federico García Lorca and Luis Buñuel

There he met other young creative students, including the poet Federico García Lorca and the future filmmaker Luis Buñuel.

Salvador began experimenting with his personal style. He grew his hair even longer and drew attention to himself with the type of clothes he wore. He was often seen in a long cape, velvet coat, and a large hat. Although he was determined to look unusual, Salvador was actually very shy.

When his classmates made fun of him, he spent time alone in the Prado Museum, copying the classic paintings of the old masters. Every Sunday, he would visit the museum. "Pencil in hand, I

analyzed all of the great masterpieces," he later said.

He also began experimenting with his painting style. A year earlier, in 1921, Ramon Pichot had shown Salvador paintings done in the cubist style.

The Prado Museum

Founded in 1819 in Madrid, the Prado is the national museum of Spain. It is one of the most famous—and important—art museums in the world. The Prado is home to drawings, prints, sculptures,

and over eight thousand paintings. There are paintings by artists like Peter Paul Rubens, Titian, and Hieronymus Bosch. But the highlight for many are the works of the Spanish painters El Greco, Francisco Goya, and over sixty works by Diego Velázquez, including his masterpiece *Las Meninas.*

Cubist painting by Pablo Picasso, 1907

This was a very modern type of painting, unlike any that had come before. Cubism attempted to show more three-dimensional images on canvas. A painting of a person or object might look more like a reassembled collage when done in a cubist style. A collage is a type of artwork in which different kinds of materials are pasted onto a surface to create a picture. One of the very first cubist paintings had been created in

1907 by another Spanish artist, Pablo Picasso.

Picasso had cofounded the cubist movement with the French artist Georges Braque. And Salvador was ready to explore the ideas of this shocking style. In 1923, he painted his own *Cubist Self-Portrait*. In this painting, Salvador's face is almost hidden in a puzzle of angles and shapes. The image is completely modern. Salvador was looking toward the future.

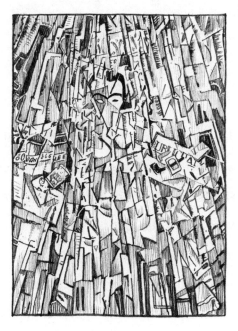

Dalí's *Cubist Self-Portrait*, 1923

Pablo Picasso (1881–1973)

Pablo Diego José Francisco de Paula Juan Nepomuceno Crispín Crispiniano María Remedios de la Santísima Trinidad Ruiz Picasso was born in Málaga, Spain. He began painting during his childhood and showed great talent early on. Picasso became a painter, sculptor, and ceramicist, whose work is identified by many "periods" including a

Blue Period, Rose Period, African influenced, and Cubist Period. Picasso spent most of his adult life in France, and that is where he created much of his art.

Two of his most famous paintings are *Les Demoiselles d'Avignon* of 1907 and *Guernica* of 1937. It is estimated that he completed around fifty thousand works of art in his lifetime! He is considered one of the most influential artists of the twentieth century.

CHAPTER 3
Troubled Student

In 1923, Salvador was part of a student protest at the Royal Academy that led to his being suspended from school for one year. He returned to his father's home in Figueres to resume his classes with Juan Nuñez Fernandez. He made time, of course, to visit the coast, where he painted *Cadaqués*, a landscape showing the trees and white sands of his beloved beach town.

There are seven women in the painting, and Salvador used his sister, Anna Maria, as the model for them all. She was the only model Salvador used at the time.

By 1924, the Spanish government was trying to ban the Catalan language—the language of the Dalí family and everyone who lived in the region. Salvador supported a political group that opposed some of the government's ideas, so he was unfairly arrested and spent nearly a month in jail. Before the year ended, he returned to Madrid, even though he was still suspended from school. After living in Madrid for several months, Salvador returned to the Royal Academy to repeat his academic year and stayed at the student residences. Once again, he spent time with his friends Federico García Lorca and Luis Buñuel, and he visited the Prado as often as he could.

In 1925, he also had his first solo show, at Galeries Dalmau in Barcelona. Although he had shown his work in a group exhibit there in 1922, this would be the first time the gallery planned to show *only* Salvador's paintings. The show was a great success! In it, he included a drawing of his family titled *Portrait of the Artist's Father and Sister*. But *Figure at a Window*, a painting of Anna Maria, is considered to be his first true masterpiece. The two artists had not yet met, but when Picasso visited the show, he remarked that this was Salvador's best work.

Figure at a Window, 1925

In April 1926, Salvador, Anna Maria, and their stepmother, Catalina, visited Paris, France. This was a dream come true for Salvador, who knew that Paris, the center of the modern art movement, was where exciting work was being created. While there, Salvador had the chance to visit Pablo Picasso at his studio.

Picasso took the time to show Salvador what he was working on and paintings that he had completed. Salvador said that visiting the great artist's studio was "as if I was having an audience with the Pope."

Just two months later, in June, Salvador was expelled from the Royal Academy, this time for good. He felt that his teachers weren't skilled enough to judge his work. In many ways, he was right. Salvador's technique was improving. His reputation was growing. He felt ready to leave school behind and begin his career as a painter.

CHAPTER 4
The Surrealist

After leaving the Royal Academy, Salvador headed back to Figueres. But he had to prove to his father that he could be a successful painter. He woke up every day at sunrise and began painting. He worked very hard to show that he had mastered the classic style of painting he had admired in the Prado. In 1926, he painted a beautiful still life called *The Basket of Bread* that shows he had mastered how to properly contrast the light and dark areas and the soft- and hard-looking

The Basket of Bread, 1926

surfaces in his work. Salvador used tiny brushes to paint so that the brushstrokes would be almost invisible. *The Basket of Bread*, like many of Salvador's paintings, looks almost like a photograph.

In 1927, he had his second show at the Galeries Dalmau in Barcelona. The paintings that Salvador exhibited now showed both realist (sometimes called "classic") and cubist techniques.

Galeries Dalmau in Barcelona

Some of the paintings also featured a new style of art known as surrealism.

French writer and poet André Breton had created the concept of surrealism a few years

André Breton

earlier, in 1924. The word means "beyond reality." The surrealist way of thinking was that dreams and intuition could unlock creative ways to make art, music, poetry, and film. Surrealist artists working in Paris at the time included the American artist Man Ray, German artists Paul Klee and Max Ernst, and the Spanish painter Joan Miró. Their idea of representing the unconscious— the part of the mind that we are not always fully aware of—appealed to Salvador. Their paintings often contained unrelated images combined in new and unusual ways.

From April to June 1928, Salvador once again spent time in Paris, where he was introduced to a few other surrealist artists by his friend and fellow artist Joan Miró. During this time, his painting *The Basket of Bread* was shown at the Carnegie Institute in Pittsburgh, Pennsylvania, and received a lot of attention. Salvador's name was now becoming known in the United States.

In 1929, Salvador helped his friend Luis Buñuel write the script for a short surrealist movie called *Un Chien Andalou* (in English: *An Andalusian Dog*). The film does not have a traditional story but follows a dreamlike series of images and characters that sometimes feel unrelated. It is based on Salvador's dream of ants crawling out of his hand, and Luis's dream of an eye being cut open. Although the film is only sixteen minutes long, it was so popular in

France, it ran for eight months at a Paris movie theater! (Many movies today only stay in theaters for about two to four weeks.) With this success, Salvador was now accepted into the surrealist group of artists.

Salvador meets Gala

After completing *Un Chien Andalou*, Salvador returned to the beach at Cadaqués in August 1929. He had many visitors there, including the poet Paul Éluard and his wife, Gala. Even though he was still a bit shy around many people, Salvador did not feel that way around Gala, a Russian woman whose full name was Elena Ivanovna Diakonova. Although she was married to Paul, Salvador could not stop himself from falling deeply in love with Gala, and the two began dating.

In November of that year, Salvador had his very first show outside of Spain, at the Galerie Goemans in Paris. He showed eleven paintings, including *The First Days of Spring*.

The First Days of Spring, 1929

This is one of Salvador's most famous early surrealist paintings. It shows scenes from his childhood against a background that is painted gray and blue. Although the show was a success and all of Salvador's paintings had been sold, his family life became a bit rocky.

Salvador's father didn't approve of his son's relationship with Gala, who was still married to Paul. He threw Salvador out of their home in Figueres and banned him from their seaside home in Cadaqués. Anna Maria stopped speaking to him. This was very upsetting to Salvador. But he was ready to begin a new life with Gala.

CHAPTER 5
Success

Because he was no longer welcome at either of his childhood homes, Salvador—along with Gala—now split his time between Paris and a fisherman's hut he had bought in Port Lligat (say: yi-GOT), a bay very close to Cadaqués.

Dalí's house in Port Lligat, Spain

On November 28, 1930, the second film Salvador wrote with Luis Buñuel, *L'Age d'Or* (in English: *The Golden Age*) opened in Paris. But by December 11, it had been banned in France. Although it  was one of the first movies with sound in that country, the surrealist comedy that poked fun at much of society was considered too shocking by many people in the audience.

The next year, the first surrealist exhibit in the United States took place at the Wadsworth Atheneum Museum in Hartford, Connecticut. Although the style of art was becoming well-known in Europe, the idea of surrealism was new in the United States. This show featured only work from European artists, including Max Ernst,

Joan Miró, and Salvador Dalí. Their paintings were now being seen in America, but the artists themselves remained in Europe.

The exhibit in Hartford was the very first time *The Persistence of Memory* was shown. It is the painting that Salvador is most famous for.

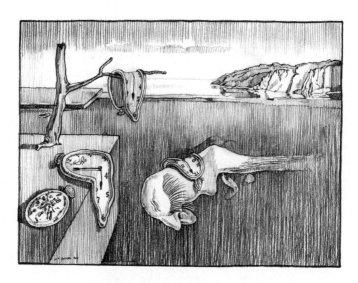

The Persistence of Memory, 1931

The images of melting pocket watches are often interpreted to mean that we cannot hold on to time, that it's melting away from us. Salvador said that it represented a dreamlike landscape near Port Lligat and was partly inspired by very soft cheese he and Gala had for dessert the night he began painting it. Although he later claimed not to fully understand it himself, it is the painting that established Salvador in the art world as a true surrealist and a master painter.

Dalí with Julien Levy

In 1932, New York became a growing source of support and financial success for Salvador. American art dealer Julien Levy bought *The Persistence of Memory*. And in November and December 1933, the Julien Levy Gallery in New York City exhibited the painting, along with the work of Picasso and other surrealists.

Americans seemed ready to embrace this new style of art and this new artist.

CHAPTER 6
"Gala-Dalí"

Early in 1934, Salvador and Gala (who had divorced Paul Éluard in 1929) were married. But their time together in Port Lligat was short. The Catalonian people revolted against the Spanish government, and the newlyweds feared a civil war might break out. Salvador was a proud Catalonian, and he understood why his people wished to  be independent, but he also knew that staying in Spain could be dangerous.

Salvador's political views often clashed with the other surrealist artists, and he was also ready to move on and try new ways to experiment with his art style. He still held a great admiration for the old masters that most of the surrealists did not. And he was open to other forms of surrealist art besides painting. He was happy to create pieces that were sometimes made from found objects. In 1933, he had created *Retrospective Bust of a Woman*, which was a combination of a female store mannequin, a loaf of bread, and corncobs.

Because of the unrest with the government and the disagreements with his friends, Salvador and Gala left for France. They did not have much money when they got there, so Pablo Picasso gave Salvador enough money to travel to the United States. In November 1934, the couple sailed to New York City. Salvador gave his first interview with American reporters even before leaving the ship. They thought he—and his paintings—

were delightfully eccentric (unusual and slightly strange). Salvador's arrival with Gala was covered in the New York newspapers the next day.

While in the United States, Salvador sold twelve paintings and gave five lectures on the growing movement of surrealism. In January 1935, Salvador and Gala were getting ready to leave New York City and return to Europe. The day before they left, the Dalís threw a fancy party and asked their guests to come dressed as their most recent dream. They called it the Dream Ball. Guests were asked to pay for their own dinner and drinks. Salvador was dressed as a corpse, and Gala wore a black headdress that held a wounded doll covered in ants.

This time, the New York reporters wrote about what the Dalís wore and the outrageous party the couple had thrown. And the international press picked up on the story as well. Now, for the entire world, the name Salvador

Dalí and the surrealism art style were forever linked.

By now, Gala was not only Salvador's wife but also his model, his business manager, and the most important person in his life. He felt so close to Gala that he even began signing some of his work "Gala-Dalí" as if they were one person.

The Angelus of Gala, 1935

In 1935, Salvador painted *The Angelus of Gala*, a double portrait in which his wife is seen both from the front and the back. When they returned to Cadaqués, Salvador and Gala received a warm welcome from Salvador's father. But Anna Maria did not feel the same way, and she spit on the floor after seeing Gala. Even though Anna Maria didn't like it, Gala was now part of the family.

CHAPTER 7
Collectible

While briefly in Cadaqués, Salvador painted a surrealist portrait of an American actress, titled *Face of Mae West Which Can Be Used as an Apartment*. This work, along with *The Persistence of Memory*, came to define Salvador as a world-class artist, and his fame continued to grow.

Mae West

He and Gala traveled much of the time, visiting friends in different European cities.

In January 1936, Salvador gave a lecture in Paris accompanied by an old woman carrying an omelet on her head. After Salvador finished speaking, the old woman poured milk onto his foot. It seemed as if nothing was too surreal—too dramatically dreamlike—for this surrealist.

In June, Salvador and Gala attended the first international surrealist show in London. The International Surrealist Exhibition was held at the New Burlington Galleries. The gallery rooms were filled with paintings by Klee, Picasso, Miró, Man Ray, and others. The show was a huge success. "Surrealism is catching on marvelously in London," Salvador wrote.

While in London, the Dalís stayed at the home of English poet Edward James. Salvador gave his host, who was a collector of art, the gift of one of the most famous surrealist objects ever made: *Lobster Telephone*. It was based on a drawing Salvador had done a few years earlier

for the magazine *American Weekly*, and it was constructed from a black rotary telephone with the plaster form of a fully cooked lobster on top.

A month later, Salvador gave a lecture wearing a heavy deep-diving suit. He was holding two dogs—large Russian wolfhounds—on a leash. He made a spectacular entrance. Salvador wanted to show, in the most surreal way possible, that he was "plunging deeply into the human mind" during his talk. But he couldn't breathe in the metal helmet. After a few tense moments, he was rescued by a workman who helped him remove it.

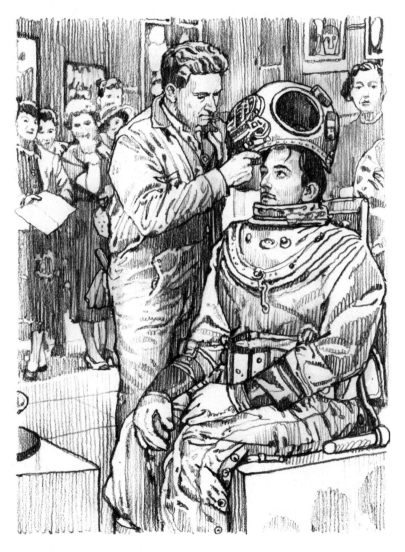

The story and pictures of Salvador in the diving suit only made him more of a star. He was now used to being in the news and being photographed. He was beginning to understand the value of his work. And he and Gala were becoming a powerful couple in the art world. They dressed fashionably in expensive clothes and ate at fancy restaurants. And they were ready to make another trip to New York.

At the end of 1936, the Museum of Modern Art (MoMA) held an exhibit called *Fantastic Art, Dada, Surrealism.* There were emotional reactions from many of the artists who had been included in the show. Although the Dada movement had influenced the surrealists, the Dada artists felt their art should not be shown alongside the surrealist work. And some of the surrealists felt the same.

Dada

The Dada movement was developed in the early part of the twentieth century by international artists who rejected standard ideas of art and wanted the people who saw their artwork to rethink the items and ideas in the world around them. The Dada artists were not only painters but poets, writers, sculptors, and collage makers.

Some of the most well-known Dadaists are Jean Arp, Marcel Duchamp, Man Ray, Hannah Höch, Max Ernst, Tristan Tzara, and Beatrice Wood. In many ways, their art challenged what the definition of "art" was and what it could be. One of the most famous pieces of Dada art is the urinal titled *Fountain* by Marcel Duchamp from 1917.

While he was in New York, Salvador appeared on the cover of *TIME* magazine on December 14, 1936. The article stated that "surrealism would never have attracted its present attention in the U. S.

were it not for a handsome 32-year-old Catalan with a soft voice and a clipped cinemactor's [movie star's] mustache, Salvador Dalí." To be featured on the cover of a major American magazine was a big achievement.

Salvador ended the year with reason to celebrate. But back in Spain, things were much less joyful. The Spanish Civil War had begun. The government had been overthrown by Francisco Franco, a dictator who would rule Spain until 1975.

Francisco Franco

Over the next three years, Figueres would become the most heavily bombed city in the Catalonia region. Federico García Lorca, Salvador's dear friend, had been killed. The Dalí family home in Cadaqués was hit by a bomb, and Salvador and Gala's Port Lligat home was destroyed. In 1937, Salvador and Gala decided to stay in the United States and headed west to California. They lived in Hollywood, a neighborhood in the city of Los Angeles, California, that is known as the home of the film industry in America.

Both Salvador and Gala enjoyed their time in Hollywood. They thought the town was full of surrealists: glamorous people who were working at making dreams into reality. They loved meeting famous actors and directors. And Salvador made important contacts in the film business. During this time, he also began writing for fashion

magazines including *Harper's Bazaar* and *Vogue.* It seemed that Americans were interested in the Spanish artist's ideas about every creative subject.

CHAPTER 8
Celebrity

Salvador and Gala returned to Europe to attend the International Surrealist Exhibition in January 1938. The show was held in Paris, and featured over three hundred paintings, drawings, sculptures, found objects, and photographs by sixty famous and lesser known artists.

For the show, Salvador provided an installation called *Rainy Taxi*. An art installation is a creative design or structure that transforms the space it's located in, usually only temporarily. Salvador's taxi was surrounded by plants and greenery. It was crawling with live snails. And, occasionally, water would fall like rain inside the vehicle. It was one of the main attractions of the International Surrealist Exhibition and showed how much Salvador's art had changed from his early years.

Earlier in 1938, the famous doctor Sigmund Freud had left Austria because of the growing threat of the Nazi government to Jewish people who lived there. Freud is the founder of psychoanalysis, a type of therapy that treats the unconscious mind. He was well-known for analyzing the dreams of his patients. In July, through the invitation of a friend, he agreed to meet with Salvador in London. Like the other surrealists, Salvador admired Dr. Freud. And now the man who painted dreams was going to meet the great man who studied and interpreted them.

Sigmund Freud

Dr. Freud spoke as Salvador sketched. Until then, Dr. Freud had thought of the surrealists as a group of foolish artists. But meeting Salvador changed his mind. He admired Salvador's energy and his drawing skills. Nothing could have made Salvador happier.

After leaving London, Salvador and Gala spent the rest of the year in Italy, where he studied art that was created during the Italian Renaissance. He closely examined and sketched classic works of art and those of the most famous Renaissance artists. He wanted to learn as much as he could about the history of Italian art. Salvador took his trips to Italian museums, churches, and archaeological ruins (buildings and items from ancient times) very seriously. He wanted to learn everything he could about them. Over his lifetime, Salvador never stopped studying the history of art.

In 1939, Salvador and Gala once again sailed for New York City. The demand for Salvador's work was growing in the United States. Soon after his arrival, he was asked to design a surrealist window display for a famous New York City department store called Bonwit Teller.

His themes for the two large windows were day and night. But when the scenes were rearranged in a way that upset Salvador, he moved to put the display back as he had intended. He accidentally broke the glass window, endangering everyone on the sidewalk who had gathered to see his work. Salvador spent the night in jail for the damage he had caused, and the New York newspapers reported that the famous artist had been jailed.

Back in Paris, the other surrealists were horrified by his behavior and the negative publicity it caused. They felt that Salvador was more interested in creating shock and anger than in taking his work seriously. But the newspaper stories worked in Salvador's favor. He became more well-known than ever. During

his show at the Julien Levy Gallery a few days after the disaster at the department store, almost every one of his paintings (including *Portrait of Doctor Freud*) sold for over $25,000. That is equal to almost $500,000 today. At age thirty-four, Salvador was one of the wealthiest young painters in the world.

Later that year, Salvador was asked to design a pavilion—a small, decorative building—at the World's Fair in Queens, New York. The theme of the fair was "the world of tomorrow," and organizations and businesses from countries all over the world set up exhibits that represented what they thought the future might look like. Salvador's surrealist pavilion included a dreamlike cave of pools, mermaids, and undersea creatures. The ticket booth was shaped like a giant fish head.

While other exhibits focused on new technology like air-conditioning and color photography, Salvador's *Dream of Venus* structure, like the artist himself, was not built to fit in.

The Italian Renaissance

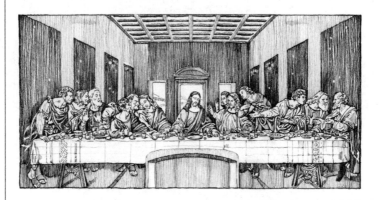

The Last Supper by Leonardo da Vinci

The period of Italian history that bridged the Middle Ages to the modern world during the fifteenth and sixteenth centuries is called the Italian Renaissance. The word *renaissance* is French, and it means "rebirth." This was a time of exploration, new ideas, and great change in scientific discovery and artistic achievement.

In art, it signaled a return to a more natural, sometimes called the "classic," style. Michelangelo and Leonardo da Vinci are among the most celebrated people of the Renaissance period because they were skilled in many areas, including painting, sculpting, and architecture (the construction of buildings). Michelangelo's sculpture of *David* and Leonardo da Vinci's painting *The Last Supper* are two of the most famous works to come out of the Italian Renaissance.

It was during a short trip back to France that Salvador began to understand the value of his name and his work as

One of Dali's perfume bottle designs

a "brand" (even eventually designing perfume bottles, costumes, and jewelry). Salvador was thrown out of the surrealist group around the time he painted *The Enigma of Hitler*. He said that it was simply based on a dream. But the surrealists thought it was shameful to paint the German dictator, even in a small image as part of a larger painting. André Breton nicknamed Salvador "Avida Dollars." This is an anagram (a rearrangement of letters in one word to form another) of the name Salvador Dalí. It is translated as "eager for dollars." Breton thought Salvador would create anything for money.

The Enigma of Hitler, 1939

And although he was not insulted, Salvador knew his days with the surrealist group were over.

In September 1939, Nazi Germany, under the leadership of Adolf Hitler, invaded Poland. The Nazi Party wanted to establish Germans as a "master race" (those who are superior to all others) and acquire a vast new empire in Eastern Europe. This was the start of World War II,

the deadliest war in history, which was fought between the Axis powers (Germany, Italy, and Japan) and the Allies (led by France, Great Britain, the Soviet Union, and the United States). Europe was no longer safe. In 1940, Salvador and Gala once again left France for the United States, where they would live for the next eight years.

CHAPTER 9
American Exile

Once back in New York, Salvador was ready
for a new start. He grew his mustache longer so
that he could twirl the ends. In a self-portrait from
1941 called *Soft Self-Portrait with Grilled Bacon,*

Soft Self-Portrait with Grilled Bacon, 1941

the mustache is exaggerated and reaches nearly to his eyes. Salvador later said that the mustache was inspired by how he wanted to be seen at the time: living a new life in America and wanting to be even more unique. The painting showed the future—the person he was growing into and the mustache he did not yet have.

In 1941, the Museum of Modern Art devoted a major show to Salvador's paintings along with those of fellow Spanish painter Joan Miró. The MoMA catalog for the show said that Salvador's work was "meaningful in [a] historic sense." The magazine *Art Digest* wrote, "Dalí steals the show." The exhibit later traveled to eight other cities around the country and secured Salvador's reputation as an artist who deserved all the attention he was getting. Salvador grew even more famous. He designed sets for two ballets at the Metropolitan Opera. He wrote his own life story, *The Secret Life of Salvador*

Dalí, which was filled with made-up stories. And he proclaimed that he was finished with surrealism.

While spending time in California, Salvador collaborated with filmmaker and businessman Walt Disney to create a short animated film called *Destino*. Although Salvador worked for months to design the art for the movie, it wasn't completed, and Disney moved on to other projects. In 1944, he worked with Alfred Hitchcock on the movie *Spellbound*, about a man who has lost his memory.

Alfred Hitchcock

The film director wanted Salvador to design special parts of the movie that would show the character's dreams. Hitchcock said, "Dalí was the best man for me to do the dreams . . . so that was the reason I had Dalí."

World War II ended in 1945 with the Allies winning. Many parts of Europe had suffered major damage due to the fighting there. People began the difficult work of rebuilding their lives after so much death and disruption. Salvador had been safe in the United States, but it was time to end his "American exile"—the years he had spent living in America.

In 1948, he and Gala went back to Spain.

Dalí's work in the movie *Spellbound*

Salvador was forty-four. His painting became much more spiritual and sometimes magical. Influenced by the time he had spent in Italy years earlier, Salvador returned to painting in the classic style and was inspired by images within the Catholic religion. He said, "To be a surrealist forever is like spending your life painting nothing but eyes and noses." It was during this time that he painted *Madonna of Port Lligat*, his first major religious painting. Gala posed as the Madonna, mother of the infant Jesus.

CHAPTER 10
The Cosmic Dalí

In 1949, Salvador's sister, Anna Maria, wrote a book, *Salvador Dalí as Seen by His Sister*, that greatly angered the famous painter. Because he felt that Anna Maria had been disrespectful to Gala in her book, he stopped speaking with Anna Maria, and with his father as well. Salvador became even closer to his wife. Later that year, he had a private visit with Pope Pius XII, the leader of the Catholic Church. This was a very important moment for Salvador. He was now introducing more Catholic images into his paintings. And he wanted to discuss his marriage to Gala. It was Salvador's wish to marry her in church, and he wanted the pope's permission.

In addition to the religious and spiritual

themes he had already been painting, Salvador became very interested in science and history. He now began to paint very large paintings of historical scenes.

When his father died in 1950, Salvador learned that he was not included in his father's will. A will is a legal document that explains what a person wants to happen with themselves and their property after they die. Salvador faced legal challenges to remove his own paintings and drawings from his father's home. But the next year, he painted one of his most memorable paintings, *Christ of Saint John of the Cross*. The crucifixion of Jesus is a popular image in Christian art. But Salvador's painting reflects his own style and dreamlike quality. The figure of Jesus is seen from high above the cross, looking down. The bottom of the painting includes fishing boats tied at his beloved Port Lligat. Although he said the idea came to him in a dream, the painting clearly shows the influence of Diego Velázquez's painting *Christ Crucified*.

Dalí's *Christ of Saint John of the Cross*

Less than five years later, Salvador painted *The Sacrament of the Last Supper*. It reminds viewers of da Vinci's *The Last Supper*, which was painted over 450 years earlier. But Salvador has combined in this large painting his ideas of mathematical principles (in the geometric shapes and composition), science, and dreams. He even included the Bay of Cadaqués in the background. *The Sacrament of the Last Supper* is over eight feet wide and over five feet tall and is now one of the most popular paintings in the National Gallery of Art in Washington, DC.

Salvador began painting one of his largest works in 1958. *The Discovery of America by Christopher Columbus*, which measures thirteen feet tall by ten feet wide, took Salvador a year to complete. (*The Persistence of Memory*, in contrast, is only nine and a half by thirteen *inches*.) Like *The Sacrament of the Last Supper*, this painting combines many ideas: Spanish history, religion, and myths. Columbus, an Italian explorer, is shown as a very young man, and his ship is painted very realistically. But the floating crosses and the mysterious background give the painting a supernatural feeling.

The 1950s were a very busy time for Salvador. He produced some of his most well-known paintings. His work was seen and reviewed all over the world. And he was able to fulfill one of his own dreams: to marry Gala in a Catholic church. Salvador and Gala had received the pope's permission to make that happen.

The couple wed in a small ceremony on August 8, 1958, in Girona, Spain.

CHAPTER 11
Reinvention

By the beginning of the 1960s, the value of Salvador's paintings had greatly increased. He was a very wealthy man. Along with Pablo Picasso, he was the best-known painter in the world. He was now as famous for his art as he was for his eccentricities—the strange things he often did to get attention. But the world was changing. And a new generation of young people embraced the publicity-seeking antics that many of Salvador's old friends had always disliked about him.

In 1965, he met the young artist Andy Warhol in New York City. Salvador had always loved the energy of the city. Both Salvador and Andy were superstars. The creative spirit at Andy Warhol's New York factory—the studio where

he made films and silk-screened canvases—was
exciting to Salvador. The parties that Andy threw,
called "happenings," reminded Salvador's admirers
of his *Rainy Taxi* and his World's Fair pavilion.

Andy Warhol's Factory in New York

Dalí with Andy Warhol

Andy said of his time with Salvador and Gala, "It's like being with royalty or circus people . . . it's not like being with an artist."

Salvador appeared on television shows and was happy to give interviews. He was in demand, not just as a great artist but as a designer and a creative thinker. He was asked to design swimsuits, ashtrays, perfume bottles, and to model men's shirts. He even created the logo for a Spanish brand of lollipops!

Chupa Chups

An internationally popular brand of lollipops, Chupa Chups was founded in Spain in 1958. The Chupa Chups logo was designed by Salvador Dalí during its first marketing campaign that used the slogan "*Es redondo y dura mucho.*" This translates in English to "It's round and long-lasting."

In 1995, Chupa Chups became the first candy to go to space! It was sent to the Mir space station with Russian astronauts, called cosmonauts. The lollipops are currently manufactured in over one hundred flavors worldwide.

Salvador's face and mustache were recognizable around the world. And he knew how to market himself as if he were a product for sale. In 1969, he took a pet anteater for a walk on the Paris Metro (a rapid train system). But it turned out that he didn't own the anteater—he had just borrowed it for the attention! He had hired a photographer to help him create this odd scene, certain that it would be printed in the French newspapers.

By 1970, Salvador began working with the French photographer Marc Lacroix, who took pictures of the painter seated outside in bright light. His photograph *Dalí Through the Eyes of a Wise Man in Morocco* is sometimes referred to as "Saint Dalí" because it looks as if Salvador has a halo. The photograph *King Dalí* shows the royal-looking Salvador wearing a crown, his mustache perfectly curled. The two men worked together on a special

Christmas issue of *Vogue* magazine that incorporates Salvador's paintings and Lacroix's photographs.

King Dalí photo by Marc Lacroix

On September 28, 1974, the Dalí Theatre-Museum opened in Figueres. The public theater there had been bombed during the Spanish Civil War. With Salvador's help, it had been rebuilt. This was the same theater where Salvador had shown his very first works as a young man, over fifty years earlier. And on that day, at the age of seventy, he was presented with the gold medal of Figueres. The museum contains some of Salvador's drawings and paintings, and a version of *Rainy Taxi* is parked there.

The Dalí Theatre-Museum in Figueres, Spain

CHAPTER 12
A Man in His Tower

Salvador and Gala now split their time between Port Lligat and the town of Púbol, nearly forty miles away. A few years earlier, in 1969, he had purchased the Castle of Púbol for Gala. It was where Gala could rest, relax, and live like a princess.

Castle of Púbol

The couple made their final trip to New York in 1979. And even though they had received their flu shots, they both became ill in early 1980. The painter, now seventy-six, and his wife, who was ten years older, were both quite frail. In April, they returned to Spain. Salvador was diagnosed with Parkinson's disease, a medical condition that affects the brain and nervous system.

Gala never fully recovered from the flu and died on June 10, 1982. She was buried at the Castle of Púbol. Salvador was physically ill and heartbroken without Gala. He was not sure how to go on living without her. He spent much of his time in bed. A short time later, King Juan Carlos I awarded him the noble title Marquès de Dalí y de Púbol, which was a great honor. And in the United States, the Salvador Dalí Museum (known as the Dalí) opened in St. Petersburg, Florida. In 1983, he managed to begin painting again. He completed his final painting, *The Swallow's Tail*, that year.

The Dalí Museum in St. Petersburg, Florida

In 1984, after a fire in his bedroom in the castle, he was admitted to a hospital in Barcelona to recover. He never returned to the Castle of Púbol. When he left the hospital, Salvador moved into a room in a tower of the Dalí Theatre-Museum. It was there that King Juan Carlos I visited him in late 1988. Salvador gifted the king what would turn out to be his last drawing, called *Head of Europa*.

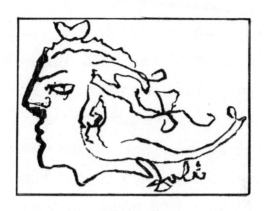

Head of Europa

On January 23, 1989, Salvador Dalí died of heart failure. His coffin was carried through the streets of Figueres, which were lined with thousands of people.

In death, the painter looked peaceful, his mustache perfectly waxed like the hands of a clock at ten past ten, just the way he liked it.

Today, Salvador's legacy lives on. The Dalí Theatre-Museum is one of the most visited museums in Spain. The Castle of Púbol is now the Gala-Dalí Castle house museum. And in 2003, the Disney film *Destino*, which Salvador began working on in 1945, was finally released.

Throughout the twentieth century, Salvador Dalí saw many art movements and styles rise in popularity. He had met nearly all the most important artists of the century—painters, filmmakers, poets, designers, and writers. Among them all, Salvador stood out. He was talented, successful, and unique. His quest to be different allowed him to become one of the most recognizable people in the world—and one of the greatest artists of all time.

Timeline of Salvador Dalí's Life

1904	Salvador Dalí is born on May 11 in Figueres, Spain
1912	Sets up an art studio in the attic of his family's home
1925	Has first solo show at Galeries Dalmau in Barcelona, Spain
1929	In November, meets Gala for the first time
1931	The first surrealist exhibit in the United States takes place in Hartford, Connecticut, featuring his painting *The Persistence of Memory*
1934	Marries Gala
1936	Appears on the cover of *TIME* magazine
1939	Designs exhibit for the New York World's Fair
	Expelled from the surrealist group
1942	Publishes his autobiography, *The Secret Life of Salvador Dalí*
1958	Marries Gala for the second time in a church ceremony on August 8 in Girona, Spain
1969	Designs Chupa Chups logo
1980	Diagnosed with Parkinson's disease
1982	The Salvador Dalí Museum opens in St. Petersburg, FL
1983	Completes his final painting, *The Swallow's Tail*
1989	Dies on January 23 in Figueres

Timeline of the World

1904 — United States Army engineers begin work on the Panama Canal

1912 — The British ocean liner RMS *Titanic* sinks in the North Atlantic Ocean on April 15

1922 — American aviator Amelia Earhart buys her first airplane

1931 — The Empire State Building is completed in New York City

1941 — Mount Rushmore is completed in South Dakota on October 31

— Japan attacks the US naval base at Pearl Harbor, Hawaii, on December 7

1952 — Elizabeth II becomes queen of England after the death of her father, George VI

1968 — The term "heavy metal" as it refers to a type of music is first used in the rock song "Born to Be Wild" by Steppenwolf

1971 — The voting age in the United States is lowered from twenty-one to eighteen

— Walt Disney World Resort opens in Orlando, Florida

1989 — East German citizens rush to the six checkpoints separating East and West Germany, leading to the dismantling of the Berlin Wall, beginning on November 9

Bibliography

*Books for young readers

*Bennett, Leonie. ***The Life and Work of . . . Salvador Dali***.
  Chicago: Heinemann Library, a division of Reed Elsevier, Inc.,
  2005.

Brown, Christopher Heath, and Jean-Pierre Isbouts. ***The Dalí***
  Legacy. New York: Apollo Publishers, 2021.

Dalí, Salvador. ***Dali by Dali***. Translated by Eleanor R. Morse,
  New York: Abrams, 1970.

Etherington-Smith, Meredith. ***The Persistence of Memory:***
  A Biography of Dalí. New York: Random House, 1992.

Friedewald, Boris. ***Dalí's Moustaches: An Act of Homage***. Munich:
  Prestel Verlag, 2016.

*Guglielmo, Amy. ***Just Being Dalí***. New York: G. P. Putnam's Sons,
  2021.

*Kelley, True. ***Who Was Pablo Picasso?*** New York: Grosset &
  Dunlap, 2009.

*Klein, Adam G. ***Salvador Dalí***. Edina, MN: Abdo Publishing, 2007.

*Wenzel, Angela. ***The Mad, Mad, Mad World of Salvador Dalí***.
  Munich: Prestel Verlag, 2007.